Awakening the Power of Self-Love: #*Secrets to Body Positivity*

The book is written by a professional who tries to help people understand their body image as understanding why we think a certain way is the first – and most crucial – step to actually changing it. Rather than focusing on what we don't like in our bodies and what we want to change. The author encourages readers to concentrate on the positive and what they can actively do and to question why they want to change to begin with.

The link between our thoughts and behaviours and how we end up feeling is made clear as it is those thoughts and behaviours that cause us to feel the way we do. The book includes personal experiences, statistics, realistic advice, techniques, methods, and steps that can be followed by anyone (even if it takes time to get used to them).

I recommend this book to all those who want to understand their body image better and how to change it in a healthy manner.

This whole book feels like a quick therapy session that could encourage you to change your whole way of life.
- Fatima Aladdin, *Reedsy Discovery Book Reviewer.*

Many people grow up with hangups about their bodies. We are our own worst critics when it comes to our body parts — for instance, your nose, your ample curves, lack of height or muscles. However, most of us outgrow these perceived flaws or, with time, accept them as what makes us unique. Yet, that doesn't mean we don't struggle with our body image from time to time, or we've forgotten being teased or bullied about our looks. Here's a question: does your body image interfere with the quality of your life? If so, then this book will help change the way you look at yourself.

Most of the information in these short eight chapters is not new but is compiled in a handy guide that's easy to read. It explains what body image is, how to set smart goals, and looks at factors contributing to developing a positive body image. Then, the author sets out the benefits of a positive role model, and offers strategies on how to build your self-esteem, and tips for self-care and self-love.

What I love about this book is the emphasis on changing your thoughts. I can relate to the struggle to change negative thoughts and feelings and appreciate the long-term goal of the practical steps. I also like the soothing statements such as "I'll be alright" or "I can do this." The strategies offered are do-able, but you'll get the most out of them by repetition. There's no quick fix to change a lifetime of self-defeating behaviour.

- Vida Li Sik, *Reedsy Discovery Book Reviewer.*

This book is written by a fellow food blogger, who you can tell has grown from her life experience when it comes to accepting her body and changing her mindset about what she believes about her body.

I particularly love the book because it's a short quick read which packs all the information you require to help you take steps towards loving yourself. The author has also included short stories that make the points discussed in the book even more relatable.

What the book does well is not just addressing the SMART goals you need to achieve body positivity but also addressing the underlying causes about why we struggle with body acceptance overtime. For example, the author includes how childhood influences can play on how we view ourselves when we become adults, she also talks about how health issues and unrealistic Western beauty standards can play a part in self-acceptance.

For me, what the book has highlighted is the need for us to unlearn bad habits which have been imposed on us unconsciously and relearn healthy habits which will bring us happiness and satisfaction from within. I love this point because the book explains how we can change our thoughts and beliefs (power of the mind) in ways that boosts our emotions, moods, and all-round physical health.

As a Mum and Fitness Content Creator, I can truly resonate with this book because the author has also designed a healthy habit journal which can help with the unlearning process.

- YummyMummy, *Food blogger and Fitness Content Creator*

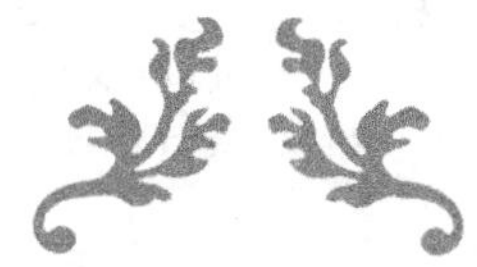

AWAKENING THE POWER OF SELF-LOVE

#Secrets to Body Positivity

By

Ayo OJ

First Paperback and Kindle Edition: March 2023

Second Paperback and Kindle Edition: June 2023

Edited by Ayo OJ and Muhammad Arslan Hafeez

Cover art and Layout by Ayo OJ

Printed by Amazon in the UK, USA and Worldwide.

Published by Ayo OJ, United Kingdom

For the people, both family and friends, who have loved me through all the different stages of metamorphosis in my life.

Most especially for my mother Funmi, my hero, and my husband Segun and my son, Gabriel, my loves. THANK YOU.

To my siblings Ayoola and Dami, and Friends Funmi, Maimuna, Lorraine and Vicky, thanks so much for always encouraging me.

To the beautiful readers who I believe will blossom as they journey through this book, YOU ARE ENOUGH.

ABOUT THE AUTHOR

Ayo OJ

Ayo is a Scientist by profession with a BSc Hons and MSc in Pharmaceutical Science, she also studied Psychology as part of her A levels at college and excelled. She has a wealth of experience and knowledge in carrying out scientific research, a technique which you will find at work in this book.

She is also a Wife and Mum, and an avid reader, who has read a lot of motivational and philosophical books. Her favorite genre of books to read are fiction, self-help, non-fiction, historical and romance.

Ayo has always wanted to be an author after first reading *'Things fall apart by Chinua Achebe'* at the age of 7 in her Grandpa's Library in *Ibadan, Nigeria*. From then on, she started thinking of ways to put her life experiences to paper. She's looking forward to not just writing non-fiction books but also fiction in the near future.

When she's not busy dreaming up the next title of her book, she loves to paint, food blog and create fun content, and she also likes to spend time with her family.

Table of Contents

I am now in my mid-30s (mind you still relatively young lol) and as I have slowly approached this age, I've come to realize that in life one can never meet up with the world's standard of beauty as it is always changing. This realization has taught me one *major* lesson in life and that is, the only way to attain true happiness about how you view yourself is to *be body positive* by *accepting yourself*!!!

For so long I have watched how Western standards of beauty has slowly eroded the confidence of both men and women worldwide and I have had first-hand experience of this.

So just a bit of a background, here we go, growing as a dark-skinned young tomboyish African girl child, I recall different people constantly feeding my young mind with a lot of negative ideas about myself, such as 'You are too skinny', 'You are too dark skinned and nobody will ever love you, so you must lighten your skin', 'You are too boyish, learn to carry yourself as a female' – Yes, you read right!! and No, I am not making generic statements or paraphrasing. These were the statements that made me lose my self-worth and confidence as a child and moving on into my teens, it wasn't any better as I was constantly bullied by my peers and every time this would happen, I would put it down to, 'I wasn't good enough' and I recall resorting to unhealthy habits such as binge eating.

It felt like my worst fears were coming true because when situations like those mentioned above would arise, my thought would always go back to all the negative words I heard growing up and I would conclude that those naysayers were correct all along. Then in my tweens, specifically age 10, I started boarding school at an all-girls school in Nigeria, where I was constantly picked on again for not looking like the other girls. These girls would usually say I was: too dark – I was called all sorts of names for this in particular, too short to dance, hadn't hit puberty right, just like they had (bear in mind that most of these girls were 13 and I was 10).

The situation changed when I started University in the UK, I had started to gain weight, my body was changing positively I thought, and it seemed for a moment that I was suddenly accepted by society. I made more female and male friends and I remember having so much confidence because I suddenly felt SEEN. This was short lived because I struggled with my weight again for an underlying reason and I now found myself constantly flashing my mind back to all those negative experiences as a child and at this point I was in my mid-20s, then it suddenly hit me that I was now owning these words which were not a true description of how I viewed myself and because of this, I started to express and carrying myself in the stereotypical manner I had been described by others all along.

I managed this underlying situation for over a decade until my health improved and now in my mid-30s I can confidently say that self-love is a choice and can be done, it just requires a bit of motivation, determination, balance, and good habits. I have also learnt that what other people say about me is their opinion and that is what it is. And it ends there.

Finally, I also figured out that learning to be confident is something I had to do by myself and that is why I have written this book, to share the tips that have assisted me in reaching this level of self-consciousness, acceptance and love that no matter what anybody says I AM ENOUGH.

INTRODUCTION

You have arrived at the first step toward developing a positive body image. This is an outstanding book meant to equip you with the necessary skills, information, and ability to think critically. The way individuals perceive themselves is referred to as their body image. This varies from having an incredibly positive body image in which an individual values their body to having a negative body image in which an individual despises their physical appearance. We are fully aware that individuals' perceptions of themselves are influenced by their body image, as our bodies are such an integral aspect of who we are.

Some people may adopt harmful eating and physical activity patterns, and dissatisfaction with one's body develops into not accepting one's entire being.

As someone who studied psychology in college, I have learned that women, men, and children struggling with body image concerns also struggle with anxieties. These issues have prompted a great number of people to experience intense concern and grief, in addition to binge eating, extreme diets, and exercises that are contributing to the deterioration of the issue.

What I've found to be valuable in my personal experience is CBT (Cognitive Behavioral Therapy), a type of therapy in which the patient's thoughts and behaviors are changed. Throughout the book, you'll see instances from people who have battled, but won, the struggle against self-abhorrence.

If you're reading this book intending to improve your life, you are not alone. According to a study of Western society, 60% of women and 30%-40% of males feel unsatisfied with some aspect of their body.

Body image is a major worry for people aged 15 to 30, and it is regarded as more important than family, friends, and school by most. Most women's concerns are centered on their weight and shape. The hips, stomach, buttocks, face, and thighs are often the most affected areas.

Men frequently express concern about muscularity, their upper body, overall body fat, and a desire to lose weight. On the other hand, body image encompasses more than appearance. It is not just about weight and size; it's also about the physical components of our bodies and our general appearance—for instance, the color of our eyes, hair, nails, and skin.

As a result, you may acquire a strong hatred for certain body areas. For women, this refers to how curvy their body is, and for men, it refers to their physical strength and body build.

A great dislike for a particular area of the body or our appearance can lead some people to obsess over the body part to the point of being dominated by thoughts of its frequently societal perceived (as opposed to objectively true) imperfection.

This can be extremely distressing and drive the individual to spend considerable time in front of the mirror or attempting to alter the perceived flaw, frequently at the expense of their mental health. Extreme self-consciousness about one's looks is a symptom of Body Dysmorphic Disorder (BDD). A psychological disorder in which a person's appearance consumes them.

I have encountered individuals that are inconvenienced by the form of their nostrils or the proximity and shape of their noses. They spend countless hours' double- and triple-checking their eyes, to the point that they waste time inspecting these locations for potential issues.

Negative feelings and thoughts about our bodies can be quite detrimental to our lives, influencing things like our health, self-esteem, anxiety levels, dietary habits, our capacity for social interaction, our mood, and our work relationships and habits.

This book is intended to benefit people of all ages who wish to know about body positivity.

Utilize this book to guarantee that you first have a positive body image and then engage in behaviors that communicate this to others, such as children who constantly monitor adult behavior. Then on to the chapter on how to assist others in developing a positive body image.

It can be challenging to enjoy life if you have a poor perception of your body. The good news is that we can alter our behavior and how we feel about our bodies, which results in a more optimistic outlook and, therefore, a fulfilling life.

You have already taken the first step in this direction. Improving your body image necessitates education on the origins of your beliefs as well as an adjustment in how you think about and interact with your body. How many of us unfairly punish our bodies and ourselves by indulging in tough exercise when our bodies need a break, starving ourselves to reduce weight, or missing social activities because we detest the way our bodies look? Body image is just one aspect of who you are, and this book will help you get the most out of it while also increasing your confidence in it and yourself. This book provides a straightforward technique to appreciating the flesh you are in.

In this book, you will learn how to alter your behavior and thought processes so that you can feel better and act in healthier and beneficial ways to your overall health. This book discusses the following topics:

- Understanding what a body image is and the variables that influence its development.
- Knowing how to change our behavior and thinking in order to feel better about our bodies and selves.
- Recognizing early warning signs of negative physical and mental health consequences, such as:
  - Eating disorders
  - Acting as a positive role model for children
  - Coping strategies for stress, anxiety, and unhappiness
  - Ways to boost one's self-esteem.

This book will teach you about body image, motivate you to think about issues that affect women, women, and children, and lead you how to improve your body image. There are ideas throughout on implementing these approaches, as it is through this habit of challenging your behaviors and thinking that you will get more significant results and long-term transformation. Furthermore, the book contains several helpful exercises for readers to try.

This book is meant to help you increase your body and life enjoyment while decreasing physical discomfort and worry by following the advised steps. It will increase your body image awareness, understanding, and comprehension, allowing you to challenge your own beliefs and habits.

Individuals who read this book will be at various phases of change preparation. You may simply be thinking of a shift; in that case, gather as much educational material as possible so that you will know what to do when the time comes.

Those willing to change and act should do the exercises as often as feasible. Change takes time, and practice is essential with any new skill. It may be difficult at first, but after a while, it will become second nature, and you will know what to do when you are in a negative body image situation. Anyone can use this book to enhance the efforts of persons who have already begun their path toward a positive body image.

Many individuals will need to repeat the methods and strategies presented in this book several times over several weeks until they become habitual and have a new way of thinking and behaving. As a result, keep up your efforts even if you don't see quick results.

Because this book is about self-care from head to toe, use the tips to improve your complete self-image rather than simply your body image. Above all, have fun with your reading and activities. Maintain a positive attitude because understanding that you can change your sentiments and ideas about your body will help you stay motivated to reach your goals. I wish you the best of luck in developing a more cheerful outlook toward yourself and your body.

So, let us get started!

Chapter 1 - WHAT IS BODY IMAGE?

Body image is a wide term encompassing both individuals' perceptions of their physical appearance and their "attitudes and sentiments about" it.

Do you have a positive attitude about your body?

Are you pleased with your appearance?

Your perception of your body is likely unique to you. For instance, when you look in the mirror, you may perceive your hips to be larger than they actually are or than other people believe they are. This is because our viewpoint is influenced by a variety of factors, including our environment, our mood, the other things we are thinking about, our level of rest or fatigue, and the food we've consumed.

As a result, what we see in the mirror is frequently not our true picture; rather, it is our shifting perception of our reflection. It is not uncommon for partners to express their admiration for their spouse's beauty or attractiveness, but the partner may not believe them. This is because our partners and friends value our positive features. Still, we are often tougher on ourselves, especially when we are sad or depressed and have had bad life experiences or trauma such as bullying. Additionally, we view ourselves through the lens of our past experiences, both positive and negative, which affect our picture of ourselves. We are frequently our own toughest critics and detractors of our own bodies. If only we could appreciate the beauty that others do.

Body image encompasses your thoughts or what you tell yourself about your body and any prejudices you may have about physical attractiveness and what constitutes true beauty.

Your thoughts and assumptions about yourself and physical appearance generate feelings about your body. For instance, you can tell yourself, "*I really enjoy how I look today in these trousers,*" leading to positive ideas about your body. You may also think to yourself, '*My arms are so flabby that I'm sure everyone in the room is gazing at them.*' I really should visit the gym more frequently,' which will make you feel horrible about your body.

Why are some people so affected by their body image that their sentiments about their bodies affect their everyday lives, while others appear to be unconcerned?

The importance we place on appearance, weight, and shape explains a great deal. For instance, if my self-esteem is based on my family and work, and both are doing well, I will feel content; yet, if my self-esteem is based on being skinny, and I believe myself to be overweight, I will feel completely miserable. And, because I'm miserable, I'm likely to stop doing activities that make me happy.

Even 'moderate' dieting increases the risk of developing an eating disorder in adolescent females. Dieting is socially acceptable, but it can have substantial physical health repercussions and most people who lose weight by dieting gain it back over time. Dieting isn't a sustainable option. Rather, focus on eating a variety of foods for nutrition and enjoyment and practicing dietary flexibility.

A woman's body image might also influence her relationship with physical activity. Women who are self-conscious about their appearance, size, or shape may avoid physical activity. This could be because they believe that being active or participating in specific activities makes their body more visible to the public.

To lose weight or change her body shape, a woman may over exercise or engage in excessive physical activity. A positive relationship with physical activity comprises engaging in regular physical activity that is both enjoyable and fascinating and is focused on maintaining or improving physical fitness. Instead of focusing on weight loss or body modification, focus on the benefits of physical activity for physical, mental, and social health.

Body Dysmorphic Disorder

Consider a brief examination of an excessive body image condition that has been clinically diagnosed. **Body Dysmorphic Disorder (BDD)** is a type of mental disease in which a person becomes obsessed with an imagined or exaggerated sense of physical imperfection. Often, there is nothing physically wrong with a person, but they believe there is.

For example, the size of someone's nose may induce them to be excessively preoccupied with the contour of a facial feature, hairline, or another part of their body. This anxiety gives the individual tremendous distress, and they frequently spend considerable time (hours) checking and re-checking this body region. This obsession can lead to the individual seeking a surgical option to resolve what they perceive to be an issue.

BDD causes social and occupational challenges for individuals since they are self-conscious and constantly preoccupied with thoughts about the body part. It is not to be mistaken with a fixation with weight or shape, which is characteristic of eating disorders.

If you believe you may be suffering from BDD, seek professional assistance. First, it is advised that you acquire a referral from your primary care physician. This condition is treatable, and sufferers should not be embarrassed to speak with a health professional. It is a very real affliction that must be managed seriously due to the significant impact on a person's life.

What Are the Benefits of Maintaining a Positive Body Image?

Positivity toward our body increases our self-esteem and overall feelings. We are more likely to make health and well-being-promoting decisions when we feel good about our bodies. We are more open to the world around us when we are at ease in our own skin. We are also more likely to work towards positive goals when we accept and feel good about our bodies.

We are more at ease socially and in public when we are happy with our bodies, and we are more inclined to jump in and accomplish things when we are at ease with our bodies.

Now that we understand what body image is and the types of ideals men and women hold, as well as some of the psychological and physical consequences of having a negative body image, we can now examine why we idealize these figures and how we can alter our perceptions and how we view our bodies in order to have a more positive image of ourselves.

Recognizing our origins is the first step toward improving our body image and healing.

A negative body image is caused by several circumstances, including the following:

- Being made fun of because of one's appearance as a child.
- Growing up in a family that places a premium on physical appearances of a certain size or shape.
- Parents and other family members who are unhappy with their appearance and participate in diets or weight-loss programs.
- A cultural tendency to judge people primarily based on their appearance.
- Peer pressure on teen girls and women to be thin, diet, exercise, and compare themselves to others exists.
- Images in the media and advertisements that promote specific aesthetic principles.
- Western media's penchant for promoting fad diets and weight loss programs.
- With the greatest of intentions, public health programs encourage people to lose weight.

Chapter 2 - SETTING SMART GOALS

When we want to make a change, we need goals, targets, and ways to track our progress. This chapter will show you how to set personal and positive body image objectives. Setting goals may appear simple, but it is a skill.

How often have we made goals only to fall short of them or abandon them along the line?

Goals must adhere to a formula for us to remain motivated to achieve them and see results right away.

Setting **SMART** (**S**pecific, **M**easurable, **A**chievable, **R**ealistic, and **T**imely) goals is the term for this. Try to produce your SMART goals before the conclusion of this chapter and keep adding to and crossing them off as you progress through this book and begin to achieve them. Some goals, such as "feeling good about my body," will be ongoing and met on a regular basis, while others will be more discrete.

When people are dissatisfied with their looks, they frequently try a variety of techniques to improve them. Dieting, excessive exercise, calorie restriction, and the usage of a variety of beauty treatments and cosmetics are examples of such practices. People will occasionally take considerable measures to improve their appearance, even getting surgery.

According to studies, changing our physical appearance, including our weight, and having surgery may not always result in a more positive body image.

How many of us have set weight-loss goals for ourselves only to fail to meet them and not feel any better, or to beat ourselves up for not being able to keep them up? According to studies, people who lose weight or make other changes to their appearance don't always have a better body image or a better mood.

So, rather than focusing on enhancing your physical appearance, try to make your goals about changing your mindset or engaging in healthy practices. Furthermore, if we want to see long-term improvements in our health and well-being, we need lifestyle-changing goals that we can stick to overtime.

Regular exercise or taking half an hour for relaxation, for example, can be sustained over time, whereas losing 10 kilos or having toned arms are very specific goals that can be achieved relatively quickly, but what can we work on in the long run?

Set goals for yourself to help you change your thinking: setting goals that will make you feel better about yourself, and your physique is a good idea. It's possible that none of these have anything to do with altering your physical look. Our goals are often unreasonable, impossible, and unsustainable if we solely focus on changing our appearance.

So, if focusing on improving our appearance does not always lead to a more positive body image, what will? Changing your attitude toward your looks and yourself, as well as the way you think about your body and yourself, is a better option than altering your physical appearance.

This mental shift will affect how you feel about yourself, your body, and your looks.

Remember that we're trying to improve our self-esteem inside and out, so think about lifestyle and health goals. The outside appearance of your body does not have to influence how you feel about it on the inside. A good example is how some people with burns or trauma can easily adjust to their new appearance and have a good outlook on life.

People whose beauty we admire, such as celebrities, struggle to be satisfied with their appearance despite having so-called "perfect" bodies. There are several examples of models and celebrities who have spoken out about their battles with eating disorders and body image concerns, and these are people whose bodies are supposed to be "ideal." Your outward appearance has no bearing on how you should feel. You can learn to accept your body for what it is, regardless of its appearance.

It's also important to remember that there is no such thing as a perfect body. There may be people whose physique or appearance we admire, but it doesn't mean we have to try to look like them, which is impossible unless you share the same genetic code.

When setting goals, it's also critical to concentrate on the good. So, when we tell ourselves we want to stop dieting, hating our bodies, or worrying about our receding hairline, we're putting a negative spin on what we're trying to do. Rather than saying, "I want to stop doing this and that," it could be better to concentrate on the positive. What do I want to do instead? We could, for example, make a goal to gaze in the mirror and focus on the things we like, eat foods that are good for our bodies, and exercise for fun. Goals that tell us what we want to do and what we'll do instead of checking compulsively, for example, can help us focus on what we're trying to do rather than what we want to stop doing.

Our body image is unique to us, shaped by unique or comparable experiences and circumstances. While two people may have a negative body image, their experiences are likely to differ significantly. The parts of their bodies that they despise will undoubtedly differ, as will the circumstances that make them unhappy. It's also likely that they have quite different perspectives and attitudes about their bodies and quite different approaches to dealing with their problems.

The importance we place on looks, for example, often determines how we are seen. As a result, you have a one-of-a-kind body image experience. The following chapter will help you understand where your body-related beliefs and feelings come from, as well as how you may tackle them in future chapters to feel better about your body.

It's worthwhile to spend some time trying to understand your own body image since the more we understand it, the easier it is to change.

What parts of your body do you find unsatisfactory?

What circumstances make you unhappy and have a negative attitude toward your body?

What assumptions and beliefs do you have about your own body and physical attractiveness in general, and how do they affect your feelings?

What are you doing to cope with these negative feelings?

Answering these questions can help you not only understand your current body image but also identify particular areas where you may need to make changes. Focusing on how you'd like to feel, think, and behave differently about and towards your body might help you achieve your goals. 'I'd like to feel more love for my stomach,' for example, or 'I'd like to stop overeating every day,' or 'I'd like to exercise for fun.' Concentrate on the things you'd like to change and frame them in a positive manner. Remember to be specific and think about how you'll evaluate the change and determine whether you've fulfilled your goals. Some activities, such as enjoyable hobbies and more exercise, may be beneficial, while others, such as overeating, starvation, and exercising just for weight loss, maybe detrimental.

Make a list of 5–10 goals you have for your body and how you feel about it and refer to it frequently while reading this book. One goal might be to quit obsessing over your weight or feeling self-conscious in public. Then, write down how you'll know if you've achieved your goal. 'If I weren't so worried about my weight, I'd spend more time with my pals,' for example. It's crucial to write down how you'll know if you've achieved your goals to keep track of your progress while you read the book.

Write down your objectives, and then write down how you expect to achieve them using the tactics and approaches as you read the book.

When focusing on your objectives, try to be as specific as possible and write them down in such a way that you will be able to tell if you have met them. You can evaluate whether you've achieved your goal of 'offering my body one compliment every day' or 'feeling less terrible about eating certain foods.' Make sure your goals are attainable as well. Setting goals like "always feeling good about my body" or "never eating unhealthy foods" may be unrealistic. Check to see if your goals are attainable.

You might want to start with some easier goals and work your way up to more difficult ones if you want to see immediate benefits. For example, you may set a goal to first understand your own body image better, then develop techniques to overcome body image worries, and lastly, feel more positive about the body part you don't like.

Chapter 3 - CHANGING YOUR BEHAVIOR AND FEELINGS

Getting out of bed and going for a walk in the morning makes me feel better about myself. Going outside in the fresh air and moving my body gets my day off to a great start. Additionally, I am aware that I have finished my regular fitness schedule! When I begin my day with a walk, I immediately feel better, and I am much more likely to adhere to my daily health goals. Numerous people struggle with their weight to the point that their bodily and mental health suffers. The most frequently given response is to 'lose weight.' This is a statement that has been made several times. As previously said, when our goal is to stop doing something, it is far more challenging to accomplish because the goal is regarded as unfavorable. When we shift the focus to something positive, such as feeling healthier and being able to walk more, people are more likely to achieve and maintain the objective.

Recognizing how our actions affect our emotions is the first step toward improving our body image. As previously stated, we frequently believe that we feel a certain way due to a particular circumstance. However, our own thoughts and behavior contribute to our feelings. For instance, two people may witness an identical event but have diametrically opposed reactions. Why? Due to the way they both perceive or think about the situation.

Have you ever noticed how different people appear to be having different experiences during a party? Some appear to be enjoying themselves, while others appear bored. They are all in the same situation, but their reactions are quite different. This is due to the inner workings of each individual's mind. Some may have recently disagreed with someone and are thinking negatively about it, while others may think about how much they enjoy party chatter and feel amazing. In contrast, still, others may be ecstatic about the event and are thus feeling positive.

Have you noticed how you might be in the same situation at various times and experience completely different emotions? The situation is identical, but you have a different reaction to it. And this is due to your thoughts, to what is occurring in your mind. As a result, it comes to reason that if we can alter our thoughts, we can alter our feelings. We frequently expect the circumstance to change, such as our boss or partner acting differently, but we can feel better about the situation by learning to think differently. The following chapter examines how our thoughts are altered. However, explore how our actions affect our feelings and how altering our conduct may result in more pleasurable sensations.

Take Care of Your Physical Appearance

There is a clear association between our actions and treatment of our bodies and our feelings about them. Have you ever noticed that when you are unhappy with your body, you punish it by overeating or undereating, skipping social events, wearing unflattering clothing, or participating in excessive exercise?

And how are you feeling as a result? Generally, it makes you miserable.

We are inflicting unnecessary pain on ourselves, which only makes us feel worse. Correct?

Consider the last time you did something negative out of frustration. Perhaps you were excessively drinking due to a breakup or a terrible event. Consider how it made you feel, and I am sure it did not resolve the issue. There was a time in my life when I was having a dreadful day; all I wanted to do was binge eat and forget my troubles. The following day, the troubles reappear. When we are anxious or tense, we must develop constructive coping mechanisms to alleviate or address the situation. There are numerous temporary fixes, such as eating and drinking, which divert our attention, but they do not address the root cause of the problem and are therefore ineffective overall.

Exercise and a balanced diet help us deal with stress and keep our minds clear, enabling us to be more effective problem solvers. Consider how you would feel if you tended to your body correctly. If you ate foods that your body appreciated in moderation, hydrated it with plenty of water, exercised with friends, dressed in your favorite clothes, gave it plenty of rest, including sleep, and avoided overworking it. You would undoubtedly feel fantastic. Consider the last positive behavior you engaged in and how you felt as a result.

Many people are ignorant that in order to feel good about their bodies, they must treat them properly. Our bodies are the only ones we have, and no one else will look after them. Today, try something kind for your body and notice how it makes you feel. For instance, you may nurture your body by bathing, going for a walk, or swimming. Occasionally, assessing your mood on a scale of 10 before and after an activity can assist you in determining what activities enhance your feel-good feelings. Appreciate what your body accomplishes for you.

Our bodies are magnificent works of art. They aid us in strolling, shopping, relaxing, sleeping, hugging, and conversing, among other activities. We usually take our bodies for granted and fail to fully appreciate the services they give. When I catch myself thinking about any flaw in my body, I remind myself that I am a beautiful and wonderfully made creature.

Consider How Your Body Functions

Consider how your body functions to gain a greater appreciation for it. I understand how challenging this is, much more so if you are injured, ill, or experiencing significant pain in your body. However, considering each body component and its function may help you shift your emphasis away from what you dislike about the way your body appears and toward how well your body performs its functions. For instance, 'I have flabby arms' to 'My arms enable me to cuddle my family.' It is what psychologists refer to as a *positive reframe*, in which you take a negative statement and turn it into a positive. Today, try it on a body part that you regularly criticize and transform it into a positive function. What positive actions can you take right now to reiterate this to yourself?

Engage in Physical Activity to Help You Feel Better

Have you ever noticed how simple things like calling a friend or leaving the house can make you feel better when depressed? Numerous studies have been conducted on the doing element and how it makes us feel better. Did you know, for example, that engaging in social activities improves your mood? Did you know that exercise can aid in the treatment of depression? What is it about doing things that elicit a sense of well-being? The causes are related to brain activation and the release of endorphins, or feel-good hormones.

When we move our bodies, we activate the brain, which increases mood due to neurochemical activity. Thus, altering your attitude toward your body is one approach to improve your self-esteem and body image. Several activities can make you feel better about your body.

Physical activity gets the blood pumping and releases endorphins or the feel-good chemicals that elevate our mood. Physical activity is another excellent way to improve your body image. If you are working toward a fitness goal, keep your attention on what you have accomplished rather than how far you still have to go. Each step advances us closer to our objective.

Take enjoyment in the present moment - pleasure is a journey, not a destination. Therefore, take delight in your journey toward your goals. Take delight in your physical activity and fitness routines. Consider how wonderful it feels to have an active body.

Make your skin feel good - treating our bodies with touch and scent (by wearing perfumes, moisturizing our skin, and shaving) revitalizes our skin and body and helps us feel better.

However, this is a highly individual decision; therefore, choose what works best for you and your body. Which scents do you prefer? Which cloth is most comfortable on your skin? When you go to bed, clean linens can feel wonderfully comfortable and luxurious against your skin, allowing you to sleep better. Get adequate sleep - sleep is critical for body and mind rejuvenation.

Eating for Emotional or Non-Nutritional Reasons

Changing our behavior in order to feel better means altering our dietary habits as well. What would happen, for instance, if you ate for your body's nutritional requirements rather than emotional ones? Apart from hunger, people consume food for a variety of reasons.

Emotional eating can occur for a variety of reasons, including sadness or suffering, boredom, happiness, anger, or worry. Eating for these reasons frequently results in negative feelings overall because we overeat and feel guilty. We believe eating will make us feel better, but it does not; it may simply confirm our lack of control over food, or it may make us feel bloated, sluggish, and less inclined to do anything else. Therefore, the next time we are sad, bored, or enraged, we should try to do something more useful. Consider the following: 'How am I feeling, and what will truly make me feel better, not only in the short term but long term?'

Chapter 4 - DEVELOPMENT OF A NEGATIVE BODY IMAGE AND OVERCOMING IT

I adore my body, for which I credit my mother. She, and my sister, regularly complimented me on how wonderful I was. My mother used to say that my grin was like turning on a light, which was brilliant and comforting because it was my kind nature that shone through. My weight yo-yoed a lot in adolescence and into my early and late twenties. If I lost too much weight and became too skinny, I was picked on, and when I gained the weight back and became borderline obese, I was still picked on by the same people, but this led me to develop some real mental health issues and negative body image. My mother, on the other hand, would explain to me that the bullies were only concerned with my size and not with me as a whole and that they do so because they suffer insecurities of their own. She was a firm believer in accepting one's physical differences. My mum helped me get through a tough time at school. She has always been a great role model. Becoming a mother and my body changing further also impacted in many ways but when I look at my child, I am grateful to my body for helping bring such a beautiful being to life.

Body image is a perspective of our physical self, what we believe we look like, and our like or dislike of it in its totality or components, as I described in the previous chapter.

Our beliefs can influence body image about our bodies and how we feel about them. The majority of people experience discontent, worry, and discomfort due to their ideas about their bodies and identities. These sentiments lead us to engage in behaviors that may or may not be healthy.

On the other hand, our thoughts are what cause us to feel the way we do. This helps to explain why two people in the same situation can have such different reactions. Despite the fact that the incident is the same, their emotions are diverse due to their differing perspectives. Let me give you an example. At the beach, two females are sunbathing and sitting on the sand. Female one is self-conscious in her swimming trunks, while female two is not. Even if the event is the same, they have distinct reactions. Why? Their viewpoints are completely opposed. 'I look huge in my swimsuit; I have a dreadful physique,' says girl one, while girl two says, 'I am satisfied with my body as it is; what a beautiful bright day.'

Factors (occurrences) that lead to the development of a negative body image.

There are numerous views about how a negative body image develops. Negative body image refers to a dislike for your entire body or certain parts of it and a perception of it as unattractive or in need of change. Whether positive or negative, body image creation takes time and starts early in life, even before we start school.

Our life experiences influence the attitudes and thoughts we have about our bodies and ourselves. Many factors frequently influence our body image. I am frequently asked by parents if they, for example, contributed to their child's eating disorder, and the answer is not always a simple 'yes.' A variety of factors have a role in the development of an eating disorder.

Let us have a look at some influences now. Understanding your body image perception, how it evolved, and what keeps it going will help you better understand your present body image. And we are much more capable of changing our body image when we understand it, how it developed, and what may be maintaining our ideas and feelings. We may understand ourselves and make essential changes with knowledge and awareness. A range of factors, including how important our body image is to us, impact how much our body image influences our daily life.

The Influence of the Society in Our Life

The way the media portrays male and female bodies, whether in magazines, on television, or on the internet, affects our ideas about how our bodies "should" look. We start receiving these signals at an early age. Certain cultural body ideals exist in all cultures. Depicting the body this way serves as a barometer for our own physical appearance. This kind of comparison is typically what makes us feel good or bad about our bodies. When we compare ourselves to an ideal image in the media, for example, we are more likely to think poorly about our bodies in contrast.

When we compare ourselves to unrealistic media images, this negative attitude is too common. For example, in modern Western society, there is a significant tendency to value women's thinness, with a slim woman typically associated with success, attention, and wealth.

A lean and muscular figure is supposed to attract ladies, prosperity, success, and pride in males. Both 'ideals' (what society considers most attractive) are impossible for the majority of people to reach. Yet, we are continually distracted with pictures of dangerously thin actors and models, and we are fed the message that only thin is beautiful or that a true man should be lean and muscular.

Furthermore, these media representations emphasize youth, and as we age, we move further and further away from these ideals, leading to dissatisfaction as we age. When making comparisons to these photos, it is crucial to be realistic. It is pointless to try to look much younger than we actually are. We may be able to appear youthful, but comparing ourselves to a late-teen image can only make us feel disappointed with our appearance if we are in our 40s, for example. As a result of these unrealistic conceptions of thinness for women and leanness, and muscularity for men, Western culture has seen a significant increase in negative body image and eating disorders. People of various ages can be affected by lousy body image, with stories of women even in their 50s and 60s having eating disorders.

Because of the optimism and normalization that these idealized representations entail, we strive for them. When we see these images in the media, we internalize them ('I have to look like that,' for example) and hence strive for something unattainable. Because it is unattainable, it frequently leads us, especially women, to indulge in harmful diets and eating habits, working diligently to accomplish the objective but never succeeding.

Failure to achieve this aim leads to a negative self-perception, negative attitudes, and beliefs, and, as a result, feelings of grief and hatred for one's body and self. This pursuit of idealized societal perceptions also explains the usage of cosmetics such as anti-aging creams, hair coloring, and hair loss therapy. Don't get me wrong, there's nothing inherently wrong with proceeding with any of these but it's the intentions behind them that matter the most.

So why do we pay so much attention to the media and allow it to alter our self-perception?

We are continually bombarded with idealized images, and resisting them is quite tough. We often compare ourselves to others and conclude there is a deficiency in our physique due to this excessive pressure on specific figures.

So, how do we prevent being influenced by these pictures in the media? We must acknowledge that natural bodies do not respond well to media representations. For example, the images we see in magazines are not of the actual person but an airbrushed, computer-enhanced, and touched-up version of the person with no defects. Understanding media images, often known as media literacy, will help you stop comparing yourself to false media representations. Knowing that these images are impossible and unrealistic can help you give up your desire to look like them.

'Even I don't wake up looking like Cindy Crawford,' Cindy Crawford famously said. She highlighted how all of her magazine photos are digitally enhanced, even after full makeup, airbrushing, and other cosmetic procedures. Another way to resist succumbing to the urge to conform our bodies to idealized images is to celebrate our age, maturity, and increase in knowledge and wisdom as we get older. Enjoying the years, we have and appreciating ourselves at any age or stage of life is part of being content with oneself.

As adults, we may choose to stop buying certain magazines or watching specific shows if we notice that they make us feel more critical of our bodies or troubled when we compare ourselves to the people in them. For example, about 6 years ago, I decided to stop watching a particular family's reality tv show or any shows relating to them because their shows laid too much emphasis on unrealistic representations of beauty and as I mentioned these are standards unattainable by most except if they undergo surgery, not only that their shows also made me feel less about my physical appearance which then led to me investing and wasting money in/on products that would never produce the desired results. You might want to think about what you read or see that gives you distress or concern, causing your body image to become negative. To enhance your attitude and positive feelings about your body, you may need to stop doing these things.

Beauty standards are preposterous and impossible for the bulk of us to achieve. While we may not have the power to change society's views, we do have the power to choose whether or not to accept them. Society's standards do not affect you unless you subscribe to them, and we can improve our body image by setting more realistic goals.

The only way to avoid submitting to media and cultural pressure is to address media depictions and their significance on looks. You, too, could begin to see people in a new light. Consider the attributes and non-appearance-related qualities you admire in others. The more you do it with others, the more natural it will feel to do it with yourself.

The Influence of Other Notable People in Our Lives

Throughout our lives, our family and friends can significantly impact our body image. For example, we may have come from a family that values physical beauty and emphasizes the significance of losing weight or looking a specific way. That of our family members may also influence our behavior. Witnessing a parent or sibling often complain about their appearance, for example, can affect how much importance we take on our physical appearance.

Seeing a beautiful family member call his/herself chubby as a child can lead you to believe there is something wrong with your looks. Different members of our families can also teach us about the importance of eating a well-balanced diet in our lives. Observing our parents' eating habits and abstaining from certain foods might embed in us dietary norms about what constitutes a portion of good or unhealthy food, making us feel guilty if we eat it.

Our upbringing frequently impacts our relationship with food; when we are taught specific dietary patterns as children, we frequently carry them into adulthood. It is a promising idea to think about the meals you eat and do not eat. Then think about if this is still applicable and healthy for you right now. Fussy eaters as adults may have developed from food aversions as children and carried them into adulthood.

Furthermore, there is considerable evidence that being teased about our appearance, whether by family members or acquaintances, has a significant impact on our body image. People who are teased about their physical appearance as children or teenagers are more likely to be unhappy with their appearance as adults. Teasing is dreadful, and it is hard not to take it personally and absorb it as our true nature.

Our Personality Is Also an Influence

Body image may be influenced by psychological qualities such as low self-esteem or being a perfectionist (where everything must be perfect or totally 'right'). While achieving a weight-loss goal or toning up a specific body region may bring a sense of satisfaction, it may also become an obsession in which no change is ever good enough. This can make people feel incredibly depressed and have a sense of failure for never being able to achieve their 'ideal' body.

We can look at our own standards of beauty and try to make them more realistic. Consider these questions: 'Why should I expect myself to live up to these standards if I do not expect others to?' Is it my perfectionism that prevents me from being satisfied with my body? How am I supposed to accept myself for who I am and even embrace my flaws?' Many people with anorexia hold themselves to incredibly high standards, feeling that they must be thin or else they are useless.

I compel them to think about what it takes to be a worthwhile person. When they start responding, they always start by identifying the features and characteristics that they have. I challenge them to reassess themselves in the absence of the thinness ideal.

What Is Affecting You Right Now?

While earlier school and home experiences and the influences of people and events can impact body image, the influences that are currently influencing us, those that are maintaining the way we feel about our bodies, are more significant.

Consider why you, as an adult, still hold the same viewpoint you did as a youngster. Consider what is now shaping your body image as a teenager. Is it a group of people you know? What are you reading or watching right now? While it is vital to becoming aware of our ancestors' influence, blaming them for body image issues will not help us fix them.
To effect any change in our body image, we must first comprehend the existing elements that drive it. Are we, for example, clinging to childhood taunts about our weight and afraid of reverting to them? Are we seeking to change our bodies' appearance in response to a previous partner's statement? Are we feverishly seeking to resurrect our youthful appearance? Understanding the circumstances that lead to our body image discomfort and anxiety, as well as the concepts and beliefs that these situations may generate, is crucial.

While attempting to appreciate the current impacts on body image, it is also crucial to understand the ramifications of these thoughts and beliefs (i.e., the sensations we feel and our behaviors).

Many habits, like drinking and eating, are repeated to make us feel better. This conduct does not fix the problem. Allow us to refer to non-resolving conduct as 'negative behavior' and ask ourselves, 'What could I do instead to make myself feel better in a way that is more long-lasting or does not have negative consequences like a hangover?'

Talking to someone frequently, properly treating your body, or getting some exercise to ease stress, for example, has a long-lasting and beneficial effect.

Eating Disorders

These are clinical conditions in which a person's weight and appearance become the primary, if not sole, focus of his or her life, causing considerable psychological and physical discomfort. Eating disorders are marked by severe self-consciousness about one's size and appearance and the way the body feels. Most people imagine an emaciated young girl when they think of eating disorders and what someone with an eating disorder looks like.

On the other hand, the reality is that many persons with eating disorders appear to be in a healthy weight range. Furthermore, many patients with bulimia or binge eating disorder may appear to be overweight. It is important to realize that being overweight has several physical effects, not only a person's weight but their behaviors and thoughts about themselves and their inner pain, define it as an 'eating disorder.'

Individuals with eating disorders can receive therapy, and it is critical to seek treatment as soon as possible. Significant irregularities in how a person regards their appearance and a self-centered focus on weight and size as a measure of their worth as a person are characteristics of eating disorders. Weight-loss activities frequently result in severe physical and mental health implications due to this shift in the emphasis placed on weight and shape. Early intervention is crucial since treating an eating disorder in its initial stages is much easier than treating it entirely. It is often difficult to think sensibly and change behaviors that have become habits and have taken over everyday life if they are left to a later stage.

The majority of people with eating disorders can trace their condition back to going on a diet, losing weight, and feeling successful as a result. They went from a sense of accomplishment for their weight loss to depression and anxiety about their bodies, food, and exercise as they continued their extreme dieting, becoming obsessed with food and weight. Women then acquire body self-consciousness and withdraw from social activities.

Unfortunately, those who have had an eating disorder for a long-time experience serious health consequences, which can be fatal for middle-aged and older women.

Although the risk of osteoporosis is higher in younger women, the lack of energy, difficulty sleeping, constant feeling of being cold, and hair loss are the most noticeable symptoms. Parents should seek help as soon as they notice their child's weight and size concerns interfere with their happiness and activities.

As previously said, only 1 in every 5 women are satisfied with their body weight, and over half of all women overestimate their size and shape. At the same time, men, on the other hand, usually underestimate their size, believing their muscles to be less than they are.

While eating disorders are uncommon in the general population, it is quite common for women to display some of these behaviors from time to time. For example, it is common for a woman to restrict her meals because she is overweight or overate the day before. Furthermore, everyone overeats from time to time. Laxatives and diet pills are used far more frequently than most people realize in an attempt to lose weight. Using this method to lose weight is dangerous and if you know anybody using laxatives for this purpose, get them medical and professional assistance as soon as possible.

Mindfulness is an effective method for minimizing binge eating because it entails focusing on what you are doing and eating and eating more slowly to avoid the 'out of control' that comes with binge eating. People often report feeling better right after vomiting, but they later report feeling weary and low on energy, which might linger for many days. This is because important minerals and nutrients are depleted when you vomit.

The body may take up to 24 hours to replenish all of the water, minerals, and nutrients lost during vomiting. Lethargy is your body's method of slowing you down in order to recover. Furthermore, vomiting can rupture blood vessels in the eyes and face, resulting in a red and puffy appearance. As a result of the force used to induce vomiting, calluses on the fingertips may appear occasionally.

People frequently tell me about eating without tasting and eating until they can no longer eat. It causes them a great deal of distress. Binge eating is common during a period of restricted food intake or dieting, and it is important to recognize that dieting might be a trigger. Foods consumed during a binge are typically high in calories ('junk food') rather than fruits and vegetables and include anything on their 'bad' list. Binge eating, which causes a person's weight to rise as a result of the enormous amount of junk food consumed, can lead to a variety of problems associated with obesity.

Diabetes, hypertension, high cholesterol, gall bladder disease, heart disease, and some types of cancer are only a few of them. One of the advantages of not binge eating is that people's weight tends to drop, making them feel more secure and confident.

Some Suggestions for Avoiding Binge Eating

- **Maintain a healthy diet:** small meals taken regularly throughout the day may be good in ensuring that your body receives appropriate nutrients and that you are never hungry, which could lead to a binge. Regularly eating small meals helps us balance our blood sugar and anxiety levels, as well as fight binge eating tendencies.

- **Avoid missing meals at all costs:** Avoid skipping meals if at all feasible. Missing a meal might make you feel hungry later in the day, leading to binge eating.

- **Have a well-balanced diet:** This helps to maintain a healthy balance of blood sugar and emotions, making you feel more stable and less agitated and so less likely to overeat.

- **Create a distraction:** It may be useful to have something else to do while you are tempted.

- **Other positive activities:** Going for a walk, interacting with friends, reading, or listening to music are all examples of this.

- **Before you overeat, think about your options:** 'Do I honestly want to do this and face the consequences?' ask yourself when the urge is particularly strong.

- **Exercise:** It may be useful to do a small amount of exercise each day. Feeling fit and active can be another motivator to avoid binge eating.

- **Keep in mind that you are in charge:** You have complete control over what you eat and do not eat. Binge eating is a sign that you are losing control of your life. As a result, get back in control by doing something other than binge eating.

- **Relax:** People frequently binge because they are anxious. Do something more relaxing instead. Reconsider if you actually want to binge by counting to ten or taking a few deep breaths.

- **Think about the ramifications**: Binge eating might leave you feeling anxious and unsatisfied.

- **Make your goal a healthy one:** Instead of declaring, "I will not binge," add, "I want to feel good; I want to feel healthy."

- **Have faith in your abilities:** Recognize your accomplishments and remind yourself that you are capable of accomplishing this assignment.

- **Reward yourself for your achievements**: Binge eating is a difficult habit to break. As a result, treat yourself to something nice for your body, such as a bubble bath, massage, or pampering, or set aside some money (that you may have spent on binge eating) for something lovely for yourself each time you control it.

Chapter 5 – ACT AS A POSITIVE ROLE MODEL FOR CHILDREN

This may be extremely valuable for teachers and other people who play a significant role in a child's life. Positive role modeling and offering opportunities for children to develop healthy and enjoyable behaviors can help you provide the greatest possible chance for your child's mental and physical health. Parents can assist their children in acquiring a healthy body image and self-esteem in a variety of ways. Speak with your child if you are concerned about their body image, self-esteem, or eating habits.

Body image formation occurs at an early age when children become aware of their own bodies. When children begin to engage with others, they develop an acute awareness of the differences between their own and others' bodies. Children learn about their bodies through their parents, siblings, and friends, as they are good observers of others. They are sensitive to their parent's reactions to their own bodies and to the perceptions of others, particularly once they attend school. This is typically the starting point for being concerned about appearance and weight.

Children face the same media pressures as adults, with commercials on television and the internet encouraging girls to be skinny, beautiful, and conform to various body ideals, while boys are encouraged to be lean and muscular. As a result, discontent with one's body might emerge at an early age. For example, as young as seven years old, it has been demonstrated that children experience body image difficulties, participate in dieting habits, and develop eating disorders.

As a youngster matures and is exposed to more influences from others such as friends, the media, instructors, and parents, they develop a greater sensitivity to body image dissatisfaction. On the other side, puberty may exacerbate a girl's negative body image, as it did me because I was a late bloomer. Physical changes like weight gain and increased body fat further distance individuals from the cultural ideal of false slimness.

As a result, educating girls about normal body growth and making comparisons to 'real' women rather than those in magazines, on the internet, or television is critical for good body image development.

Parents, for example, can sit with their children and discuss what they see and think, as well as correct any misunderstandings or attributions. Around adolescence, girls develop an increasing sense of insecurity about their weight and may begin dieting and striving to lose weight. They observe others, such as their parents, peers, and teachers, and access a wealth of information on the internet.

The majority of this information is unfiltered and useless. Parents should be on the lookout for dissatisfaction with one's body image during adolescence. It can result in hazardous behaviors such as eating disorders, depression, and anxiety, particularly among teenage girls. This is not to say that all teenagers will have a bad body image (many will be content with their appearance), but it is a time of notable change as they transition into adulthood.

The following tips will assist your child, regardless of age, in developing a positive body image to the greatest extent feasible.

Being a positive role model for your child is the most effective way to instill a healthy body image in them. You are your child's most influential role model. Parents may demonstrate to their children how to feel good about themselves. Children, for example, imitate their parents' eating habits – what you eat, they will imitate. Children are good observers of adult behavior; therefore, if you' diet' or eliminate certain items from your diet, your children will wonder why and what is wrong with you. My mum was a body positive role model for me growing up, she was comfortable in her skin and with that she would dress and carry herself with so much confidence, that I remember then as a 7-year-old child, I wondered if she was born on Venus. I remember also watching her have a healthy habit, where after her meal, she would eat fruits and have a glass of juice and few hours later go for a walk, a habit she still does till date.

Avoid instilling a good/unhealthy food dynamic in children, as this may worry if they consume anything that is not on the good list. It may be more advantageous to discuss food in terms of its effect on and in the body, such as how food fuels the body to enable us to play, learn, work, sleep, and rest. For instance, you could talk with your child about which foods provide energy and aid in thinking and which provide a boost in their wellbeing or leave them feeling lethargic. Modeling eating behavior in relation to mood can also help educate children on how to control their emotions positively.

Demonstrating that rather than eating or drinking when unhappy or in a foul mood, you can do something that will make you feel better, such as exercising, doing something nice, or speaking with someone. As a result, youngsters will cultivate healthy habits. Encourage your child to follow your example and create a list of things to engage in when they are bored, nervous, sad, angry, or experiencing any other emotion. Accept yourself for your unique body type and size. Because you are the living embodiment of how you like your child to feel and act, this is an effective method of teaching children about body acceptance.

Rather than complaining about areas of your body that you despise, concentrate on an aspect of your body that you appreciate. Concentrate on its function and the amazing things it accomplishes for you, such as supporting you in walking and making sitting more comfortable. Accepting other people's physical sizes and forms is also critical, as is refraining from judging others based on their looks. It is a wonderful way to avoid body image issues, provided you do not place an excessive amount of emphasis on physical appearance.

If you do need to lose weight for health reasons, make it a point to stress it and explain your actions to your child. 'Mummy has to watch what she eats more closely because she's trying to take care of her heart,' for instance. You can mention how everyone's needs vary according to their ages and phases of life. They do not need to worry about anything except eating a variety of meals and engaging in lots of physical activity to be happy and enjoy life right now. If you set a good example for your children, they are more likely to follow suit.

With a critical eye, examine media messages. Develop the ability to examine media images critically and to discuss them realistically. Discuss the issues using images that promote obesity or poor health. This same method can also be used to address anything hazardous that the media portrays as positive.

Encourage your child to question and criticize Western society's limited 'beauty standard.' Discuss the rarity of supermodels and how celebrities use make-up and airbrushing before a photoshoot to appear 'perfect,' but they are not. Discuss individuals they know and the characteristics they admire in them, such as their personality, abilities, and kindness.

Assist your child in gaining confidence. Self-esteem is contingent upon a strong feeling of identity and self-worth in your child. Assist them in realizing their true selves and abilities. Praise your child's efforts and successes, particularly if they are still in the learning process. By promoting problem-solving, expressing opinions, and being unique, you may help your child develop their ability to think for themselves and feel in control. Teach your child a variety of coping mechanisms (such as walking away, telling an adult, relaxing, and thinking positively) to assist them in overcoming life's problems, such as bullying at school. Teach them to speak up if they believe they have been treated unfairly by others.

Positive parenting's objective is to support and nurture children while also leading them in the right direction.

This instills in your child a sense of self-worth. Pay attention to your child if they come to you with concerns about something, particularly their appearance. If they are going through physical changes, reassure them and congratulate them on entering adolescence or maturity.

We should be proud of our diversity. Encourage them to interact with a variety of youngsters who have a variety of different body forms and discuss how wonderful it is to be unique. Make no mockery of a child's appearance. Make no jokes about someone's weight, body type, or attractiveness. Even seemingly innocent nicknames might be detrimental if they focus exclusively on a child's physical characteristics. If you are concerned about your child's weight, for example, for health reasons, rather than focusing just on the child, urge the entire family to live a healthy lifestyle.

Simultaneously, emphasize their accomplishments in other areas and assign them domestic chores that will make them feel included and helpful.

Consult their school. Your child's school can be an amazing place that fosters a positive self-image and body image. Any concerns you may have should be brought to the attention of your principal/headteacher or your child's teacher. They are there to aid your child in developing into the best person possible. For instance, schools should have effective procedures in place to address bullying.

There is no reason for your child to be bullied or harassed; it is not a normal part of the development and can have long-term implications. Inquire whether the school has implemented any positive body image campaigns, and if not, whether they would consider doing so.

If you believe you have thus far been a less-than-ideal role model for your child, try not to be too hard on yourself. You can make a difference starting today. There are numerous reasons why we have negative attitudes about our bodies, and focusing on improving your own body image will attract children's attention and help them learn to love their own bodies as well. What resources are available to me? If you have concerns about your child's body image or self-perception, it is preferable to get therapy as soon as possible before the issue becomes serious.

Chapter 6 - COPING STRATEGIES FOR STRESS AND ANXIETY

Certain situations make us uneasy and self-conscious about our bodies. If we cannot prepare for them ahead of time, we need 'quick relief' strategies or ways to regulate our anxiety, as psychologists call them. While we may not be able to completely eliminate anxiety, we can certainly reduce it or make it more bearable. The following are a few quick-relief methods:

Soothing Statements: 'I'll be alright' or 'I can do this' are examples of soothing statements we can say to ourselves. Which of the following statements are most effective for you? Consider what you told yourself when you were worried in the past. If you feel self-conscious, tell yourself, "No one is staring at me," or repeat the word "calm." Consider situations in which you have successfully dealt with adversity; use this experience to help you relax and think more clearly. You could request the help of a partner or a friend to remind you of your reassuring remarks or declarations about your abilities to deal with the circumstance.

Breathing: slowing down your breathing as much as possible and inhaling and exhaling the same amount of air as you exhale can help your body relax physiologically. Furthermore, concentrating on your breathing might help you redirect your attention and relax your mind. While repeating your relaxing statements, inhale for four seconds, hold for two, and exhale for four. Continue for at least two minutes, or until you are more relaxed. It is impossible to panic or grows irritated while your breathing is under control. Practice this in non-anxious situations so you can use it right away in a stressful situation. The goal is to keep your breathing steady and in control while focusing solely on it.

Focus: Attempting to focus on your surroundings and shifting your attention away from yourself is what it means to be attentive. Suppose you are nervous at the pool in your swimsuit because your body does not look like that of Kim Kardashian and start to feel awkward or frightened that others are staring at you. Instead of focusing on the negative or worrisome thoughts that are racing through your mind, concentrate on what you are doing, seeing, hearing, smelling, and tasting. This is a component of mindfulness; you are concentrating on the present moment rather than on the troubling notions in your head.

Rather than being overwhelmed by your ideas, it can sometimes be good to focus on what you can hear, see, feel smell, and taste. This is a particularly effective method for those of us trying to pay more attention to what we eat. Slowing down and focusing on the process of eating, including the smell, taste, and texture, can help us stop binge eating by drawing our attention to what we are doing.

Consider devoting more than 20 minutes to a meal. This means eating slowly, and focusing completely on the sensations, tastes, smells, looks, and noises of eating. Remove any unnecessary distractions, such as the television, and focus exclusively on the task at hand. One of the problems with binge eating is eating mindlessly and without consciousness. This mindful eating method will help you appreciate your meal more, give your stomach time to communicate to your brain when it is full and make you more aware of what you are eating.

Confronting your beliefs while you are self-conscious can be good in this scenario since it seeks evidence against your irrational and/or distressing thinking. If you are worried that everyone is staring at you, search for evidence; you might find that, for the most part, no one is.

Pre-conditioning your body and mind is one of the preventative strategies for anxiety control and discomfort reduction. Prepare yourself if you know you are going to be anxious in a situation ahead of time. Reduce your anxiety in the days leading up to the event. What are your alternatives? What can you say to yourself to make you feel better? This is a great chance to practice facing your self-defeating negative ideas. 'What am I scared of?' and 'Is this a rational or illogical fear?' are two questions to ask yourself. Is it likely that this worry will come true? What is the evidence for and against?' 'How can I replace this thinking with something more soothing, relaxing, realistic, and beneficial?'

Many people find that relaxing on a regular basis helps them deal with their anxiety. Relaxation may take the form of sitting quietly, going for a stroll, or listening to soothing music for some, while it may take the form of progressive muscular relaxation for others. Lowering our heart rate and calming our minds are both parts of relaxation.

Chapter 7 - BUILDING SELF-ESTEEM

Self-esteem refers to how we perceive and feel about ourselves. Our body image and perceptions have an impact on our self-esteem. How we feel about our bodies influences how we feel about ourselves. We can all improve our self-esteem in order to feel healthier and happier.

We are constantly overgeneralizing, catastrophizing, thinking in black and white terms, and so on. Take, for example, a person who believes, 'I'm no good at my job,' a more balanced perspective may be 'Today I'm experiencing difficulty with this task at work; that doesn't mean I'm not good at my job in general,' I may say if I were looking for proof. 'I'm making big assumptions here.' 'I'm struggling with this one project, and it's making me doubt my skills at work, but it's only one task; it doesn't make me a bad person overall.'

Managing Depression and Achieving a Feeling of Balance in Your Life

Dissatisfaction with one's body commonly coexists with despair and anxiety. We are much more likely to have body image dissatisfaction and feel negative about our bodies when we are depressed. As a result, learning to feel good about your body is a crucial element of feeling good about yourself overall. There will always be times in our lives when we are not in the best of moods. This could be due to stress, tension, or unwelcome news, as well as a lack of sleep, insufficient nutrition, or hormonal imbalances. The most important thing to remember about mood management is to try to figure out what is depressing your mood and then figure out what you can do about it. If it is due to hormonal swings in women, or if you are unwell, you may just have to wait it out, knowing that it will pass in a few days. For example, two of my mood lifting activities are painting, I'm quite good at drawing and painting on a canvas, and running my food blog - *@thecooking_addict* if you are interested in checking it out.

Other times, you may wish to relax or utilize coping strategies such as talking to someone, doing something you enjoy, or doing something that distracts you from your bad thoughts. If you see cognitive errors or negative thinking, apply the techniques we have taught in this book, such as reviewing data and approaching problems more rationally. If you are experiencing difficulty, seek help. Remember that a poor mood is just that, and it may happen to the best of us at any time for no apparent reason.

If your bad mood lasts longer than two weeks, it is a good idea to get professional help from your doctor, especially if it is depression or a medical or mental health condition.

Someone with high self-esteem likes himself; therefore, it is especially important when we are feeling down on ourselves to remember how valuable we are and not let our bad mood make us feel bad about ourselves in general.

Engaging in stress-reduction activities is also important for helping us feel in control and reinforcing that we are capable people. We can always increase our self-esteem, and you might want to think about where your self-esteem is lacking and how you might be able to improve some critical areas, such as:

Physical

Food, water, exercise, and overall health are all essential. These are our most basic needs, and if they are not met, they can cause tremendous stress and anxiety. Although money cannot buy happiness, it can cause stress if you do not have enough of it or are under a lot of financial pressure. In order to feel better, you must evaluate how you may improve your financial circumstances. If you are not in good health, it might impair your mood and make it harder to have high self-esteem. For example, if you need to enhance your health, work on it to boost your self-esteem and stress management.

Intellectual

This includes cognitive stimulation or doing something that pushes your mind. Learning a new skill, reading, discussing a topic in a book club, completing Sudoku and puzzles, or doing anything else that challenges your intellect are all examples. For example, simply reading this book satisfies an intellectual need.

Social

It is all about engaging with and being in the company of other people. Others help to lift our spirits, make us feel connected, and provide a significant source of stress relief. Reconnect with friends if you have been a little distant lately. Participating in team sports, joining a gym or club, and meeting coworkers for coffee can all help you reach your social objectives.

Having opportunities to smile and be validated by others is critical to our self-esteem. Simply saying hello to our neighbors or being in the company of others, such as attending a neighborhood event, might satisfy our social requirements.

Emotional

Finally, we require relaxation, rest, and enjoyment in order to maintain a sense of balance in our lives. We can meet our emotional needs through interacting with others, particularly through touch, conversation, and having people in our lives who listen to and respect us. We need time to ourselves where we may be free of stress and focus on our own needs. It is difficult for busy people to prioritize their needs, especially when they are balancing family, work, and relationships, but it is vital; we are no help to anybody else if we are not healthy enough to care for ourselves. Emotional needs can also be met by doing things we enjoy, so making time during the day for ourselves, even if it is only 20–30 minutes, is critical.

So, look over the areas mentioned above and make a list of what you do each week or day to meet these needs. If one is missing, consider how you may include it into your regular routine. When we focus on all of these areas, we are taking care of ourselves as a whole and are much more prepared to care for others. Taking care of all of these needs in yourself helps you cope in life and establishes your sense of worth and value as a person.

Chapter 8 - TIPS FOR SELF CARE AND SELF LOVE

The first step toward better health is to appreciate yourself. It is time to change the narrative if you are self-conscious about your appearance. This means acceptance of your entire body.

It begins with your thoughts, then words and action. You spend more time with yourself than anyone else, and how you treat yourself can make or break your long-term relationship with yourself.

There is no such thing as a perfect moment or weight when it comes to enjoying yourself and your body. There is only one chance, and we have the option of letting go of all the conditional love that keeps us apart.

Accept that you do not always need permission from others to be confident and assertive.

It takes time and effort to cultivate body positivity and self-acceptance. You are not alone, and you can start cultivating self-love right now.

Your self-care and self-love practices will vary according to your needs and interests, and they will undoubtedly require experimenting with new things to see what sticks (at least at first). To get you started, here are nine suggestions:

1. Begin A Journaling Exercise

Routine writing can assist you in discovering more about yourself and teaching you to value yourself. Additionally, it enables you to document your worried thoughts and sensations and monitor your progress over time.

2. Slow Down

It is all too easy to become absorbed in your daily to-do list and continue working until the day is over. Rather than that, make rest a conscious part of your life. Even if it is as simple as lying down or sitting quietly for five minutes between tasks, try to relax, enjoy some mental quiet, and carve out some space for yourself.

3. Make Time for Family and Friends

Make a list of the people with whom you are most at ease and reflect on the last time you spoke with each of them. Can you contact and invite any of those persons to chat or meet (safely)? Spending time with friends and family is crucial for your general health and investing in those relationships.

4. Utilize Mantras/Affirmations

Mantras or affirmations are phrases that you repeat to yourself repeatedly until they become automatic. For instance, you can use the phrase "I am growing" to reassure yourself that what you are experiencing is normal. You may even seek out a creative motto to guide your work.

5. Be Consistent with Your Boundaries

Take note of your own requirements. Take some alone time if you need it. Do not attempt to pretend to be someone you are not to conform or fit in with. Maintain your tranquility.

6. Meditate or pray

Numerous techniques exist for meditation. Some people meditate or pray while sitting, while others meditate or pray in bed in the mornings, with or without their eyes open. When confronted with a stressful circumstance, meditation and prayer assist in relaxing the mind and making it easier to maintain a peaceful state of mind.

7. Switch Your Phone to Airplane Mode

Numerous individuals report feeling less anxious after intentionally disconnecting from social media or their phones. Consider switching your phone to airplane mode or moving it to a different room while working or spending time with people to prevent distractions.

8. Dispose of Anything That Isn't Beneficial

Consider your surroundings. Is it brimming with objects that evoke beautiful memories and make you happy? If not, it may be time to do an inventory and get rid of things you keep around out of habit. If you feel very daring, try a minimalism challenge to determine how much you genuinely possess.

9. Choose Foods That Nourish You Internally

Just like you want your exterior environment to make you happy and feel gorgeous, you want your body's dietary choices to be kind. Everyone's dietary preferences and demands are unique, but in general, aim for a range of primarily unprocessed fruits, vegetables, grains, and proteins, with the occasional necessary indulgence.

PRACTICE OF REALISTIC GOALS CREATES A HEALTHY HABIT

What can you do with your newfound confidence?

As with any advice often given to us in life, the only way to allow them have a positive impact in our life is to ensure that we consistently practice them to ensure they become part of our daily habit or let's say a ritual. Remember that whatever goal you set yourself with regards to achieving body positivity and satisfaction must be realistic, and can be done in stages because this is the only way you can ensure that you maintain it in the long term.

What I can also advise you to do with your newly found confidence, is to flaunt it for yourself and not to appease others.

Also, if there's anything I'd like for you the reader to take away from this book, it's that you can do it and *you are enough*.

I'm particularly glad that I have been able to finally put into words all the tips and wisdom I have about helping you become body positive.

To further encourage you on your journey of self-love, I have designed a fun journal, '52 *Weeks of Body Positivity*' (also available on Amazon) to assist you with practicing realistic goals which when done overtime will become healthy habits that you can sustain.

I hope more than anything this book has helped you view yourself in a more positive light.

FURTHER RESOURCES THAT HAVE HELPED ME

1. *12 Rules for Life: An Antidote To Chaos* by Jordan Peterson

2. *The Power of Now: A Guide to Spiritual Enlightenment* by Eckhart Tolle

3. *The Untethered Soul: The Journey Beyond Yourself* by Michael A. Singer

ENDNOTES

What Influences Body Image? – BALANCE eating disorder treatment center. BALANCE eating disorder treatment center. (2022). Retrieved from https://balancedtx.com/blog/what-influences-body-image.

Body image: What is it, and how can I improve it? Medicalnewstoday.com. (2022). Retrieved from https://www.medicalnewstoday.com/articles/249190#negative-body-image.

Kuzma, C. (2022). *The 6 Factors that Can Affect Your Body Image.* Women's Running. Retrieved from https://www.womensrunning.com/health/wellness/factors-that-affect-body-image/.

Positive Self-Image: How to Improve Self- and Body-Image. Cleveland Clinic. (2022). Retrieved from https://my.clevelandclinic.org/health/articles/12942-fostering-a-positive-self-image.

Signs of Eating Disorders: Types and Symptoms. WebMD. (2022). Retrieved from https://www.webmd.com/mental-health/eating-disorders/signs-of-eating-disorders.

Anorexia nervosa: Symptoms, causes, and treatment. Medicalnewstoday.com. (2022). Retrieved from https://www.medicalnewstoday.com/articles/267432#what-is-it.

What is an Eating Disorder: Types, Symptoms, Risks, and Causes. Eating Disorder Hope. (2022). Retrieved from https://www.eatingdisorderhope.com/information/eating-disorder.

5 Ways to Promote a Positive Body Image for Kids. ParentMap. (2022). Retrieved from https://www.parentmap.com/article/how-to-be-a-body-image-role-model-for-your-child.
How to Teach Your Child Body Positivity. Mental Health America. (2022). Retrieved from https://mhanational.org/blog/how-teach-your-child-body-positivity.

5 Ways to Promote a Positive Body Image for Kids. Eatright.org. (2022). Retrieved from https://www.eatright.org/health/wellness/your-overall-health/5-ways-to-promote-a-positive-body-image-for-kids.

8 ways to manage body image anxiety after lockdown. Theconversation.com. (2022). Retrieved from https://theconversation.com/amp/8-ways-to-manage-body-image-anxiety-after-lockdown-162224.

Body Image and Social Anxiety. Eating Disorder Hope. (2022). Retrieved from https://www.eatingdisorderhope.com/treatment-for-eating-disorders/co-occurring-dual-diagnosis/anxiety/body-image-and-social-anxiety.

Body Dysmorphic Disorder: Symptoms, Causes, Diagnosis, Treatments. Cleveland Clinic. (2022). Retrieved from https://my.clevelandclinic.org/health/diseases/9888-body-dysmorphic-disorder.

Body Image and Self-Esteem (for Teens) - Nemours KidsHealth. Kidshealth.org. (2022). Retrieved from https://kidshealth.org/en/teens/body-image.html.